Anxiety and Panic Attacks

Anxiety Management. Anxiety Relief. The Natural and Drug Free Relief For Anxiety Attacks and Panic Attacks

By John McArthur and Cheri Merz

Warning

All treatment of any medical condition (without exception) must always be done under supervision of a qualified medical professional. The fact that a substance is "natural" does not necessarily mean that it has no side effects or interaction with other medications.

Medical professionals are qualified and experienced to give advice on side effects and interactions of all types of medication.

Table of Contents

What is Anxiety and Panic

Anxiety is that natural state of mind that alerts us to potential danger, whether that danger is from having left the stove on when we left the house or noticing that we are in near proximity to a dangerous animal. Anxiety has a role to play in our lives, and as long as we have only a healthy and rational level of it, it does not affect our health. However, when we become obsessed with a danger that is very unlikely or not real at all, anxiety disorder is a deadly enemy and can lead to its near cousin, panic disorder.

Imagine a scene of acute embarrassment in a public place; let's say Wal-Mart with your two-year-old, who is throwing a tantrum to end all tantrums. A normal person would be anxious to stop the racket, embarrassed to be the cause of the scene, and probably angry with the child. However, she would not avoid Wal-Mart in the future or refuse to take her child there ever again, because it would be irrational to assume that the same scene would always happen there. A person with anxiety disorder might do both, seeking to control the circumstances and therefore not experience the embarrassment again. A person with panic disorder might find herself in acute physical distress, often to the point of fainting, if she ventured into Wal-Mart with or without her child, because the environment might suddenly trigger an attack. A particularly insidious form of panic disorder, agoraphobia, would prevent the person from entering the doors of Wal-Mart at all; and perhaps from leaving her house. From the point of view of the person who has never experienced these feelings, this example may seem trivial or silly. However, similar feelings arising from any combination of risk factors may consume the sufferer's life, have a grievous affect on her health and even affect her family in numerous ways.

Almost everyone has experienced or will experience some kind of anxiety. In fact, there are several types of anxiety, which we will explore in a moment. Glossophobia, the specific fear of public speaking, affects up to 75% of all adults and some say that it is worse than the fear of death in most of those individuals. Certainly, that would account for a great deal of anxiety in some portions of the population. Nevertheless, many of the same individuals who fear public speaking worse than death manage to give book reports, sales presentations, teach in front of a classroom and even entertain the masses without ill effect. However, millions of people around the world experience severe anxiety on a daily basis with little or no reason.

According to the Anxiety and Depression Association of America, Anxiety disorders are the most common mental illness in the U.S., affecting 40 million adults in the United States age 18 and older. That amounts to about 18% of the U.S. population. The Centers for Disease Control 1 estimates the worldwide lifetime prevalence of anxiety disorder at over 15%, while the 12-month prevalence is more than 10%. That means that over the lifetime of the current population, roughly speaking, a staggering 700 million people will lose at least some of their health, productivity, and sometimes their lives, to this invisible disease.

Add to the human cost the financial cost. Anxiety disorders cost the U.S. more than $42 billion a year, almost one-third of the country's $148 billion total mental health bill, according to "The Economic Burden of Anxiety Disorders," a study commissioned by ADAA (The Journal of Clinical Psychiatry, 60(7), July 1999).

More than $22.84 billion of those costs are associated with the repeated use of health care services; people with anxiety disorders seek relief for symptoms that mimic physical illnesses. People with an anxiety disorder are three to five times more likely to go to the doctor and six times more likely to be hospitalized for psychiatric disorders than those who do not suffer from anxiety disorders. According to the same article at CDC, anxiety disorder goes hand-in-hand with depression, as nearly one-half of those diagnosed with the latter are also diagnosed with anxiety disorder.

There is no single cause of anxiety disorder, as they develop from a complex set of circumstances and risk factors, including genetics, brain chemistry, personality and life events. Although we will discuss the different types of anxiety and panic disorder in more detail in a later chapter, medical professionals understand that certain types of anxiety disorders can run in families, particularly Generalized Anxiety Disorder (GAD), Obsessive-Compulsive Disorder (OCD) and Social Anxiety Disorder (SAD, but not to be confused with Seasonal Affective Disorder). Life events can result in Post-Traumatic Stress

Disorder, with which we are all familiar concerning veterans who have been in combat situations. PTSD can also come from rape, witnessing a violent crime, physical or sexual abuse and any number of other harrowing events, both short and long term in duration.

The general symptoms of anxiety disorder include first and foremost, excessive worry. Emotional symptoms that spill over into physical manifestation include sleep disturbance, ritualistic behavior, fear of being alone or fear of being in public places, irritability, distraction and great apprehension concerning loved ones' welfare. Although several of these symptoms can occur in anyone at any time, the sufferer of anxiety disorder experiences them relentlessly.

Associated physical symptoms include heart palpitations, shortness of breath, racing pulse, rapid breathing, sweating, dry mouth, fatigue, indigestion, irritable bowel syndrome, light-headedness or dizziness, numbness and tingling of the hands and feet or cold, clammy hands. As you might imagine, many of the physical symptoms can add to the distress of the emotional or mental symptoms, setting up a feedback loop that makes the disorder grow worse without treatment.

Many treatment options are available, ranging from mind and body work, herbal therapeutics and nutrition to a wide variety of pharmaceuticals. As with many other ailments that have both physical and mental elements, conventional medicine and alternative medicine disagree on those that are most effective. A balanced approach, combining both medical camps, may be the best. If alternative therapies can improve the brain chemistry or alleviate the symptoms and underlying causes of the anxiety, it may be possible for patients to eliminate or at least cut down on pharmaceuticals, which tend to be addictive and sometimes exacerbate the very symptoms they are designed to alleviate. However, if you were currently taking any such medications, it would be extremely dangerous to your health to stop taking them unilaterally, without your doctor's approval. Instead, use some of the suggestions for naturally improving your health that follow, and seek your doctor's counsel when you feel you may be able to cut back on your medications. Always speak to a pharmacist before combining pharmaceuticals with natural herbs, as interactions could be disastrous.

Types of anxiety and panic

We have already touched on some of the different types of anxiety and panic, but it would be remiss of us not to describe more thoroughly all the recognized varieties, including their specific symptoms. Note that it is very likely that more than one is present in any individual who suffers from any of them.

GAD, or General Anxiety Disorder

People who suffer from generalized anxiety disorder (GAD) live life daily with exaggerated worry and tension about health issues, financial issues, family problems, or difficulty at work. They anticipate disaster and even just the thought of daily activity induces anxiety. A diagnosis of GAD is likely when a person worries excessively about a variety of everyday problems for at least 6 months.

People with GAD can usually function socially and hold down a job when their anxiety level is mild. They do not normally avoid certain situations, except perhaps the most anxiety-producing ones such as public speaking. They usually realize that their anxiety is out of proportion to the situation, but they cannot seem to stop the cycle of worry. If, or perhaps we should say when the anxiety level is severe, GAD patients can have difficulty carrying out even the simplest of daily activities.

Mental symptoms include the inability to relax, an overactive startle reflex, and difficulty concentrating. Often they have trouble falling asleep or staying asleep. Physical symptoms often accompany the anxiety, including headaches, muscle tension, muscle aches, fatigue difficulty swallowing, trembling or twitching, irritability, sweating, nausea or frequent elimination needs, lightheadedness, breathlessness and hot flashes.

According to the National Institute of Mental Health GAD affects about 6.8 million American adults. It affects nearly twice as many women as men. Research suggests that the disorder develops gradually and can begin at any point in the life cycle, although the years of highest risk are between childhood and middle age. There is evidence that genes play a modest role in GAD, making it more likely that an individual will develop it if other family members have it.

GAD rarely occurs alone, but is often accompanied by other anxiety disorders, depression or substance abuse, and commonly more than one of these. Conventional treatment is medication or cognitive-behavioral therapy; however, treatment of the other conditions that may accompany it with their appropriate therapies is also necessary.

Panic Disorder

Perhaps one of the most debilitating and life-disrupting anxiety disorders is panic disorder. According to the NIMH, panic disorder affects about 6 million American adults. Again, it is twice as common in women as in men. Late adolescence or early adulthood are the most common time for panic attacks to begin, but not everyone who has a panic attack will develop panic disorder. Many people have just one attack and never have another. There is evidence that the tendency to develop panic attacks may be inherited.

Most of us have heard of someone who, thinking he was having a heart attack, went to an emergency room only to be told it was a panic attack instead. The anecdote usually implies that the episode was not serious after all. However, nothing could be further from the truth. While a heart attack might be a one-time occurrence that can kill you, medical advances have given us reason to hope that treatment will be successful and there will not be a recurrence.

On the other hand, panic disorder can devastate the sufferer for a lifetime if not successfully treated. It is a real, and serious, illness characterized by sudden attacks of terror, usually along with physical symptoms of a pounding heart, sweatiness, weakness, faintness or dizziness. In addition, nausea, chest pain or smothering sensations may occur, along with flushing or chilling as well as tingling or numbing of the hands. Sufferers have described a sense of unreality or a fear of impending doom or of losing control. In other words, very similar symptoms to those of a heart attack, for men (women's symptoms of a heart attack tend to be different, but presented with symptoms such as these, women also fear they are having a heart attack.) Instead of fearing that they are having a heart attack, people having panic attacks may fear that they are losing their minds or are on the verge of death from unexplained causes.

Because it is difficult to predict when or where an attack will occur, many patients worry intensely and dread the next attack, contributing to their general anxiety. Panic attacks can occur at any time, even during sleep. They typically peak within about 10 minutes, but severe cases of the disorder may produce attacks that last much longer. People who have repeated full-blown panic attacks should seek treatment before they begin avoidance coping techniques, which can be very disabling. If you were to have a panic attack in an elevator and subsequently fear elevators, it could affect your choices in where you live, work, see your doctor or enjoy entertainment.

Agoraphobia is a severe form of this coping technique. When a patient's life has become so restricted that they avoid normal activities, sometimes to the extent of becoming housebound, they are have agoraphobia, defined as a fear of open spaces. Early treatment can often prevent agoraphobia, but panic disorder may sometimes be difficult to diagnose. It is not uncommon for sufferers to go from doctor to doctor or visit the emergency room repeatedly before someone correctly diagnoses their condition, a situation made all the more unfortunate by the fact that panic disorder is one of the most treatable of all the anxiety disorders. Most cases of panic disorder respond well to medication or cognitive psychotherapy, which helps change thinking patterns that lead to fear and anxiety.

Like other forms of anxiety disorders, panic disorder frequently occurs with other serious problems, such as other types of anxiety disorder, depression, drug abuse, or alcoholism, all of which need to be treated separately.

Obsessive Compulsive Disorder (OCD)

OCD affects about 2.2 million American adults, according to NIMH. As with other forms of anxiety, OCD can show up along with other anxiety disorders, particularly eating disorders, and depression. Unlike the forms we have discussed already, OCD strikes men and women about equally. It also shows up a little earlier, appearing in childhood, adolescence or early adulthood. Research has shown that about one-third of adults with OCD developed symptoms as children, and that OCD might run in families.

The name of this anxiety disorder springs from the two main issues. Upsetting thoughts that persist and cannot be tolerated (obsessions) lead to the individual developing rituals, or compulsions, to attempt to control the anxiety. For the OCD patient, the common anxiety that she has left the stove on when leaving the house might cause her to develop a ritual of always checking the stove precisely three times each time she leaves the house, even if she had not used the stove that day. What stems from an awareness in mentally healthy people that they have been absent-minded and had better make sure, in the OCD patient becomes something she is compelled to do. No amount of trying to talk herself out of it helps; in fact, it produces more anxiety. One young woman, concerned about germs, washed her hands so frequently that they became rough and as red as if she had held them under boiling water for several minutes. Because her hands were painful, she attempted to overcome the compulsion, with the result that she became even more compelled to do it. These rituals give their performers no pleasure and at best only temporary relief from the anxiety that stems from their obsessions.

Some rituals are less harmful, but no less annoying, for example, counting steps, actions, or just counting for no particular reason, or touching things in a particular sequence as a talisman against the anxiety. Although the rituals are relatively innocuous, they can stem from very disturbing obsessions, commonly having thoughts of violence, upsetting thoughts about sexual acts or harming loved ones. Hoarding is a symptom that the person may have OCD, as is an abnormally rigid preoccupation with order and symmetry, compelling the person to constantly straighten items on a desk, for example.

As you read this, you may think, 'Well, I check my stove before I leave the house, and I straighten the items on the coffee table. Do I have OCD?' The key to recognizing the difference is that people with OCD perform their rituals even when they interfere with daily life and even when they hate and resist the repetition. Most adults with OCD realize what they are doing, but most children and even some adults may not recognize that it is not normal behavior.

Oddly enough, symptoms may come and go, obsessions may disappear and rituals may change, depending on the individual, the severity of the anxiety, and the other accompanying pathologies. Very severe OCD can be disabling, preventing the sufferer from working or carrying out normal adult responsibilities. Like sufferers of panic disorder, they may attempt to avoid situations that trigger their obsessions, or self-medicate with alcohol or illicit drugs.

Certain medications or exposure-based psychotherapy are commonly used to treat OCD successfully. For people whose OCD is resistant to conventional therapies, research continues into combination and add-on treatments, as well as deep brain stimulation.

Post-Traumatic Stress Disorder (PTSD)

NIMH indicates that PTSD affects about 7.7 million American adults. However, it can occur at any age, including childhood. Although we are constantly reminded that returning war veterans are subject to PTSD, again women are more likely to develop it. There is some evidence that vulnerability to the condition may run in families, and again depression, substance abuse, or one or more of the other anxiety disorders often accompany it.

The trigger for developing PTSD, as one might surmise from the name, is a terrifying event or ordeal involving physical harm or the threat of physical harm. However, the sufferer may not have been the victim of the harm. It could have been a loved one or a stranger. It could have happened in an instant, as in the recent Boston Marathon bombing, or over a long time, as with child abuse. As we mentioned earlier, having been in close proximity to a war zone, even if one were not personally involved in the fighting and especially if one were involved, is a very common trigger. Traumatic incidents such as rape, torture, being kidnapped or held captive, mugging, horrific accidents involving cars, planes, subways or trains, and natural disasters such as floods, tornadoes and earthquakes can all produce PTSD in the susceptible individual.

Symptoms of PTSD include an overactive startle reflex, emotional numbness, loss of interest in things in which the person used to find pleasure, irritability, aggressiveness, even violence. They may withdraw from friends and loved ones, and have trouble feeling affectionate. Avoidance coping techniques keep them from enjoying holidays that may be in proximity to the anniversary of the event, or the anniversary may cause them to become despondent, angry or fearful. They avoid situations that are similar to the circumstances surrounding the original event. Symptoms seem to be worse for people whose triggering event was deliberate and directed at them personally, for example, an assault as opposed to a weather disaster.

The trauma that triggered an individual's PTSD may haunt the person's thoughts every day or recur often in nightmares. We call these recollections of trauma 'flashbacks'. It used to be a common misconception that flashbacks were always a full-sensory reliving of the incident. Books such as UNTIL TUESDAY, the autobiography of a war veteran and PTSD sufferer who found comfort and a degree of peace in a service dog's presence, have disabused us of that notion. Flashbacks may consist of any, some or all of images, sounds, smells, or feelings. They may cause the person to lose touch with reality and react as if the trauma were happening again, or by freezing and blanking out for a few moments. Flashbacks can be triggered by similar sounds. For example, a car backfiring down the street may trigger a flashback to the sound of gunfire. A child who unexpectedly finds himself in the presence of his abuser may lose control of his bladder or bowels. While the movie situation of a war veteran suffering from PTSD walking into a public area with a gun and mowing down innocent bystanders may be a little over the top, flashbacks can present a grave danger to the person who is having one, by robbing him of the ability to correctly see, interpret and respond to events around him.

Symptoms of PTSD usually begin within three months of the triggering event, but occasionally come out years later, perhaps after a suppressed memory is recalled. A PTSD diagnosis requires that symptoms last more than a month, and the course of the ailment varies from six months to chronic. Conventional treatment may consist of psychotherapy, medication, or both. As mentioned above, some sufferers are finding a degree of relief in the companionship of an animal that has been specially trained to be aware of its master's emotional shifts and to provide protection and comfort during flashbacks.

Social Anxiety Disorder (SAD) also known as Social Phobia

We turn now to a disorder that, while it may not have the emotional impact of PTSD, nevertheless affects up to 15 million American adults. Men and women suffer varying degrees of this anxiety about equally. Like OCD, it usually has its roots in childhood or early adolescence. Genetic factors may be involved, and self-medication with drugs or alcohol is common, which may lead to depression and substance abuse disorders.

SAD is not just a condition of being shy, it is an overwhelming anxiety or excessive self-consciousness in everyday social interaction, and occasionally can even affect how people behave in their own homes. You will find people with social phobia anxiously looking around them to make sure no one is watching or judging them. Rather than a general discomfort, this is a result of intense, chronic and constant fear that their appearance does not measure up, or that they will do something to embarrass themselves. They can worry about an upcoming situation such as a job interview until they work themselves into a state of panic.

The condition can become severe enough to interfere with work or other activities that requires the sufferer to be in the presence of strangers. It can also interfere with a person's close relationships, when the partner or spouse becomes impatient with what seems like a trivial excuse for not going out or engaging in a recreational activity like dancing, swimming or the like.

Most people with SAD recognize that their fears are unreasonable, and some can even joke about it. However, they are helpless to overcome their feelings, and even if they force themselves to enter into situations that trigger their anxiety, they will not enjoy themselves, or as in the case of a job interview, will not be able to perform well. They usually have a great deal of anxiety beforehand, cannot overcome their discomfort during the event and will worry and second-guess their behavior and actions for hours or days afterward. It may be that only one particular situation triggers the anxiety, or it could be so broad that the person becomes a virtual hermit, interacting with no one except his family without anxiety.

Physical symptoms of social phobia include blushing, difficulty talking, sweating profusely, nausea and trembling. To make matters worse, people with social phobia feel as though everyone is looking at them when the symptoms occur.

Specific Phobias

Common phobias such as the fear of flying, of spiders, of elevators and other irrational fears are perhaps the most prevalent result of anxiety disorder. Fortunately, for victims of specific phobias, the anxiety is usually very targeted, and may be relatively mild compared to some of the other forms of anxiety disorder that can severely disrupt normal life.

The most common coping technique for these phobias is avoidance. If you were afraid of small, enclosed, dark places, for example (claustrophobia), you would do your best to make sure you were never in a small, enclosed, dark place. Furthermore, you might be able to overcome your anxiety and discomfort if it were important and unavoidable, say, you might have to get into an elevator with several other people if you worked on the 20th floor of an office building. If you were afraid of flying, you might find alternative means of transportation, like sports-caster celebrity John Madden.

While some people with specific phobias can avoid the trigger or alleviate the fear with medication, alcohol or simple courage, others can become severely disabled and an unexpected encounter with the object of fear may cause distressing physical reactions. One woman, repeatedly traumatized by her older brothers with harmless snakes, became so afraid of all snakes that she could not see one, even in a photograph or cartoon drawing, without feeling faint and nauseated, and her family knew not to say the word in her presence because it would elicit a startled shriek from her every time.

Phobias can respond very well to specific psychotherapeutic intervention.

What are the signs and symptoms?

By now, even if you do not have anxiety disorder, you may be wondering if you do. Maybe you always feel you should check to see if you have turned off the stove, the lights, or the TV before you leave your house. Maybe you are a bit anxious when anticipating a flight in a plane, or a speech you must give soon. Perhaps you are apprehensive about your teenager getting behind the steering wheel for the first time.

The truth is that everyone feels some anxiety, rational or not, and the level of anxiety varies from person to person based on many factors. The first time you give a speech, you may find it hard to control your voice, difficult to hide your shaking and be very reluctant to stand in front of an audience. In fact, it may take several speeches to learn to control or not feel these symptoms. However, eventually you will have done it enough to shake off the symptoms, and if you are lucky, you will no longer have them. The difference between normal anxiety and anxiety disorder is that unless the latter receives appropriate treatment, you will never reach a place of comfort with any of the situations that trigger your anxiety. In addition, most of the triggers are irrational, having no basis in reality or, in the case of PTSD, long over.

Signs that you may have anxiety disorder are many and varied. Constant, unrelenting thoughts about the object of your anxiety, often interfering with sleep, are the most obvious. If you develop rituals in an effort to relieve your anxiety, such as repetitive hand-washing or compulsive counting, you may have anxiety disorder. You may have a form of anxiety disorder if you are unable to stop worrying about the welfare of your children, spouse or other loved ones as long as they are not in your presence. Other signs are impatience, easy distraction, fear of non-threatening situations (like being in a public place) or objects and sleep disturbance. Note, however, that some of these signs can be induced by use of controlled or illegal substances, illness not related to anxiety disorder or states of exhaustion from some other cause.

Physical symptoms that often accompany the signs of anxiety disorder are sweating, shaking, shortness of breath, hot or cold flashes, heart palpitations and other forms of discomfort. As before, all of these symptoms can also come from other illnesses. In fact, the most common reaction to a panic attack that has the elements of shaking, heart palpitations and shortness of breath, is that the sufferer must be having a heart attack. This can be very disconcerting for both the patient and immediate bystanders.

If you suspect that you have an anxiety disorder, it is necessary to separate normal anxiety-producing circumstances from excessive reaction and consider health symptoms in the light of testing for other health conditions. When all else has been ruled out, you can begin to try different therapies to alleviate your symptoms.

The side effects of anxiety and panic

Anxiety disorder and panic disorder can be highly disabling. Imagine the inconvenience if you were unable to set foot outdoors. You would need someone to shop for you, run errands for you, even bring your mail in from the mailbox. A doctor appointment would be a major undertaking. Forget family gatherings, weddings or funerals, you will not be attending. The implications are staggering, and yet that is the case for an estimated fifteen (15) million Americans aged 18-54 in any given year. Imagine the lost productivity for that many adults, not to mention the medical costs! Saddest of all is the depression that inevitably follows. Suicide is a very real threat, especially when an agoraphobic patient experiences isolation from family and friends, who often do not understand or accommodate the need to stay connected with someone who cannot contemplate leaving their home. And this is only one aspect of anxiety disorder! As we have seen, there are no fewer than six specific types of anxiety disorder, each with its own set of symptoms and challenges.

Substance abuse is a particularly insidious side effect of anxiety disorder. In an attempt to self-medicate, many people turn to alcohol or illegal drugs to relieve their symptoms. Consider the person with SAD, or social anxiety disorder. Maybe you know many of them, most of whom may not even have been diagnosed. How many of your friends and loved ones cannot conceive of going to a party or other function without taking a drink? How many feel compelled to take that drink before going to work? How many DUIs and consequent injury or deaths have their roots in SAD? It is hard to say, but worth considering. Naturally, substance abuse has its own set of attached illnesses, too. Alcoholism and its travelling companion, cirrhosis of the liver, for example.

Side effects are not limited to those that the patient has. Families are distressed, if not devastated, when anxiety and panic attacks disable a loved one. Re-read the first paragraph in this section, this time from the point of view of the patient's spouse, parents or siblings. Imagine if you were the one who was required to visit a shut-in relative every day to bring food, check the mail and make sure that your loved one was not falling into deep depression. How would it affect your life? Would you have time for yourself or other members of the family? Truth be told, it might just send you into depression yourself! Heaven forbid that your loved one attempts suicide. The ripple effect of an individual with anxiety and depression can cast a pall on an entire extended family.

Aside from the discomfort of symptoms, the disability and other illnesses that come with severe anxiety and the distress to friends and family, anxiety and panic can have long-term medical consequences from the constant stress. In fact, some of the symptoms associated with GAD and panic disorder may actually be the symptoms of associated stress. While stress is not a disease, it can cause or contribute to diseases such as gastritis, IBS, hypertension and neuromuscular disorders.

It is generally accepted that stress increases susceptibility to illness, suppressing the immune system and leaving the individual susceptible to immune-related disorders and cancer. Stress contributes to poor sleep habits, which directly affect a surprising array of health functions mediated by adrenal, pituitary and thyroid hormones, among others. It also depletes the body's reserves of biochemical components that fight infection.

It could be a matter of debate whether stress causes anxiety or vice versa, and perhaps there are valid arguments on both sides. What is beyond question, though, is that if you are constantly subjected to anxiety-producing situations, you will inevitably become stressed. Given the fact that the most prevalent form of anxiety disorder is social phobia, it stands to reason that some of the high levels of stress we are seeing in the American population these days may stem from something as simple as being forced to commute to work with thousands of strangers every day. There have been numerous experiments involving the psychology of animals and humans in overcrowding situations. One such experiment concluded that beyond optimal levels of crowding, social breakdown and illness occur. Quoting from The Ohio Journal of Science, "Crowded animal populations often show a breakdown of normal social behavior, with increased aggression and violence, aberrant sexual activity, improper parental care, and abnormal states of activity, aggregation, or social withdrawal. A variety of stress related diseases and mortality patterns may ensue." Note that the consequences listed are all potential triggers for various forms of anxiety disorder, as well.

Conventional Treatment Options

Drug Therapy

As noted in the discussion of the various types of anxiety above, many respond favorably to drug therapy with anti-anxiety or ant-psychotic medications. This tends to be the first thing that many Americans consider when faced with uncomfortable symptoms. However, these medications cannot cure the disorder; it can only relieve the symptoms. For many sufferers, this is life changing, allowing them to function normally in spite of their illness.

The three most common types of medication used to treat anxiety are anti-depressants, anxiolytics (anti-anxiety medications) and beta-blockers. Anxiety disorders are associated with certain chemicals in the brain known as neurotransmitters. These chemicals are responsible for, among other things, an individual's sense of well-being and the ability to relax. Anti-depressants and anxiolytics work by affecting the balance of one or more of these chemicals.

Beta-blockers work by blocking receptors that are associated with the physical symptoms of anxiety.

Antidepressants

SSRIs

SSRIs, or selective serotonin reuptake inhibitors, are one class of anti-depressants used to treat panic disorder, obsessive-compulsive disorder, social anxiety disorder, general anxiety disorder, and PTSD. This class of anti-depressants works by blocking the re-absorption of the neurotransmitter serotonin, thereby changing the levels, which helps the brain cells send and receive chemical messages. This in turn boosts mood. The 'selective' part of the name refers to the fact that these medications do not seem to affect other neurotransmitters, only serotonin, the 'feel-good' neurotransmitter. Brand names of medications in this class include Celexa, Lexapro, Prozac, Paxil, Zoloft and Symbyax.

These medications are considered relatively safe and reportedly have fewer side effects than other types of anti-depressants. Nevertheless, side effects do occur in some patients, and can be severe. They include nausea, dry mouth, headache, diarrhea, nervousness, agitation or restlessness, reduced sexual desire or difficulty in reaching orgasm, inability to maintain an erection (erectile dysfunction), rash, increased sweating, weight gain, drowsiness and insomnia. More disturbing, some SSRIs have been implicated in teen suicide. In 2010, the US Food and Drug Administration forced manufacturers to re-label Celexa, Lexapro, Luvox, Paxil, and Zoloft to include a warning that they may contribute to teen suicide or violent behavior. The FDA does not approve their use in patients under 18.

Tricyclic Antidepressants

Tricyclic antidepressants, or TCAs, work by increasing levels of two neurotransmitters (serotonin and norepinephrine) and blocking a third, acetylcholine. As with SSRIs, achieving a different balance of these brain chemicals may alleviate depression. TCAs are used to treat panic disorder, PTSD and general anxiety disorder. In addition, one specific TCA, Anafranil, may also be used to treat OCD. Some of these uses are off-label; i.e., not approved by the FDA. Brand names of drugs in this class include Anafranil, Asendin, Elavil, Norpramin, Pamelor,

Sinequan, Surmontil, Tofranil and Vivactil. Side effects are blurred vision, dry mouth, constipation, weight gain or loss, low blood pressure on standing, rash, hives, and increased heart rate. These drugs can also cause increased incidence of seizures in patients with seizure disorder, and withdrawal symptoms including dizziness, nausea, headache and restlessness. As with SSRIs, they can also increase suicidal thinking and behavior in children or adolescents. SSRIs have largely replaced them in treating depression, but they may have specific advantages in treating some forms of anxiety.

MAOIs

Monoamine oxidase inhibitors (MAOIs) have been used to treat panic disorder, social anxiety disorder and PTSD. They are the oldest class of anti-depressant medications and have serious contraindications for use now that newer medications are available. People taking MAOIs have dietary restrictions against foods containing tyramine (an amino acid), such as cheese and red wine. They are also unable to take ibuprofen or acetaminophen pain relievers, most allergy and cold medications and some herbal supplements. All of these substances can cause dangerous increases in blood pressure when they interact with MAOIs. In addition, MAOIs can also interact with SSRIs in a serious condition called 'serotonin syndrome', a potentially life-threatening condition that can cause hallucinations, confusion, seizures and changes in blood pressure or heart rhythm as well as increased sweating and muscle stiffness.

SNRIs

Similar in action to SSRIs, SNRIs act on both serotonin and norepinephrine, with similar results. They are used to treat panic disorder, obsessive-compulsive disorder, social anxiety disorder, general anxiety disorder and PTSD.

Anxiolytics (Anti-anxiety medications)

Benzodiazepines

Benzodiazepines are a class of medication that are effective in treating several conditions, primarily anxiety. Researchers have not discovered the specific mechanism, but all benzodiazepines affect gamma-aminobutyric acid (GABA). GABA is a neurotransmitter like serotonin and norepinephrine. GABA reduces the activity of nerves in the brain. Scientists think that excessive activity in these nerves are a possible cause of anxiety, therefore they believe that reducing this activity will also reduce anxiety. Brand names of benzodiazepines most commonly prescribed for anxiety disorder include Xansa, Librium, Transenna, Velum, and Aptiva. Side effects include dizziness, weakness and unsteadiness in addition to sedation. Benzodiazepines can also cause a feeling of depression, headache, sleep disturbance or loss of orientation. All benzodiazepines can cause physical dependence, and stopping them abruptly is not recommended as it can cause withdrawal symptoms that are more or less severe, based on how long the medication has been taken. Abrupt cessation of the medication after a few months of daily therapy may cause a feeling of loss of self-worth, agitation and insomnia. If it has been taken for longer, suddenly stopping therapy may cause seizures, tremors, muscle cramping, sweating and vomiting.

BuSpar

BuSpar (brand name) is an anti-anxiety agent that is not chemically related to any of the medications described so far. It is used to treat general anxiety disorder. Its mechanism of action is unknown. Serious side effects can include allergic reaction, feeling light-headed, fainting, fast or uneven heart rate, depressed mood, unusual thoughts or behavior, lack of balance or coordination. More likely are less serious side effects, including drowsiness, dizziness, blurred vision, feeling restless, nausea, upset stomach sleep problems (insomnia) or trouble concentrating.

Beta Blockers and Other Medications

Beta-blockers are used to treat the physical symptoms associated with performance anxiety (a type of social anxiety disorder) and sometimes for panic disorder. They work by significantly reducing the adrenaline response that produces symptoms such as pounding heart, increased respiration, sweating and cold or clammy hands. Although the FDA does not officially approve them for anxiolytic use, they have been widely used for this purpose over the last 25 years, and many drug trials have borne out their effectiveness in reducing performance anxiety. Actors, musicians, public speakers and dancers have relied for years on these medications to avoid stage fright. A list of possible side effects that includes all previously mentioned side effects and more would legislate against their use for any but the most severe cases. Brand names of these medications commonly used for performance anxiety include Propanalol, Atenolol and Pindolol.

Antihistamines, because of their sedative effects, can be used to treat general anxiety disorder, and alpha-blockers are used to treat PTSD, specifically for nightmares. Other anti-convulsant and anti-psychotic medications are used as augmentation therapies to enhance the response to other medications or mediate their effects.

As always when one reads a list of the side effects of these drugs, we must ask if the treatment is not worse than the disease. Medications, by definition, interfere with the natural workings of the human body in one way or another. It is not possible to interfere with your body's natural processes without creating some imbalance in another process. If you have ever known someone whose medications included a cocktail of anti-depressants, anti-anxiety medications and others, you will have seen that these drugs are difficult to manage. Dosage is trial-and-error, and often a physician will prescribe a drug to counteract some of the effects of the first drug, rather than working to find a more effective dose. By the time the patient has emptied her bank account buying more and more prescriptions, the array of side effects she may be experiencing simply adds insult to injury. While these observations are true, it is also important to remember that unsupervised cessation of these medications can have grave consequences. Always consult with your doctor before stopping your medication or adding supplements, as some medications can interact with supplements with harmful results.

Psychotherapy

Certain forms of psychotherapy, with or without medication, can relieve some symptoms of some of the types of anxiety. We will explore these modalities next.

The three most common types of psychotherapy used for treatment of anxiety are behavioral therapy, cognitive therapy and CBT, or cognitive-behavioral therapy. Behavioral therapy focuses on reducing the unwanted behaviors associated with the anxiety or providing the patient with coping techniques such as relaxation or deep breathing to counteract the physical symptoms associated with the anxiety. Cognitive therapy focuses on helping the patient understand and modify their thoughts and beliefs. CBT blends the two approaches, and focuses on helping the patient understand the relationship between their thoughts and beliefs and the behavior that results.

Exposure therapy is a type of behavioral therapy that has seen success in overcoming anxiety. There are three types of exposure therapy, which can be used together or separately. The three types are in vivo (real life), imaginal and interoceptive. With in vivo therapy, patients receive exercises to help lessen the irrational fear. For example, a person with OCD and an excessive fear of germs might be encouraged to get her hands dirty and wait longer and longer to wash them, in other words they expose themselves to the feared object in a controlled environment until the fear is extinguished. For imaginal therapy, patients imagine a situation in which they would normally experience anxiety, such as making a public speech, or confronting someone who has intimidated or made them fearful in the past. This type of behavioral therapy is useful for people who need to confront feared thoughts and memories. Interoceptive therapy is for sufferers of panic disorder and PTSD, who fear the physical symptoms of their anxiety as much as they experience the emotions of the trigger event again.

Each of these therapies can be found to be more effective for specific types of anxiety disorder than for others. For example, in vivo exposure therapy seems to be more effective in reducing the symptoms of generalized anxiety disorder (GAD) than imaginal therapy. Exposure-based therapies, specifically imaginal therapy, is also highly effective in treating specific phobias and is the most validated treatment for phobia. One study cited a finding that four years after a single 1-3 hour session, 90% of patients exhibited significantly reduced fear, avoidance and overall level of impairment, while 65% exhibited no symptoms of a specific phobia. One such phobia that can be treated with this therapy is agoraphobia. You will recall that we discussed the disabling consequences of this disorder a few sections back. The author has personally seen the most devastating effects of agoraphobia in a family member. To think that an exposure therapy session of only a few hours potentially could have avoided the emotional misery of a sixteen-year affliction, had the family only known of it, is very painful.

A more modern application of exposure therapy is Virtual Reality Exposure (VRE), which has shown great promise in treating PTSD. Testing of this therapy has been carried out with active-duty military personnel, and resulted, as self-reported, in greatly diminished symptoms. Further, VRE also seems to be effective in treating accompanying substance abuse.

Cognitive therapy on its own seeks to help the patient identify and change dysfunctional thoughts and beliefs. In addition, the therapist helps the patient develop skills to modify those beliefs, identify distorted thinking and identify with others in ways that are more functional. Treatment is a collaborative effort between patient and therapist to test the patient's assumptions and challenge the distorted, unhelpful and unrealistic thought patterns. This identification and challenge makes the emotions and thought patterns easier to change. There are several thought patterns, also called cognitive distortions, which can make a patient magnify anxiety-producing situations. This creates a feedback loop that eventually results in anxiety disorder when the patient is unable to let go of the thoughts.

Arbitrary inference, wherein the patient draws a quick conclusion without evidence is one such unhelpful thought pattern. This might lead to a belief that someone, or everyone, dislikes the person, when in fact there is no evidence to support such a belief. Another unhelpful pattern is selective abstraction, which means that the patient develops a belief based on one piece of evidence or one event, but ignores related information. In this case, the belief that someone dislikes him might be based on a glimpsed frowning facial expression during a conversation, ignoring the rest of the conversation during which the other person was smiling or laughing. These cognitive distortions can lead to or exacerbate GAD and SAD.

Over-generalization is the belief that because one action or event went badly, any repeat performance will also go badly. A famous example of this distortion made it impossible for the American singer Barbra Streisand to perform in public for many years. Always subject to stage fright, Miss Streisand froze on stage when she lost track of the words of her song for a moment. The more she frantically searched her mind for the words, the more awkward the moment became, until she fled the stage in horror. Until she received treatment for the disorder and returned to the stage for live performances (using a teleprompter to be sure it did not happen again), her career was stalled.

Other cognitive distortions include personalization, wherein you arbitrarily attribute someone else's mood to something you have done; dichotomous thinking, otherwise known as black and white, wherein you only recognize the extremes of a situation; and labeling, wherein you attach a negative label to yourself based on one situation, for example, you trip and label yourself awkward. Once again, these types of thought patterns are not uncommon; it is when you obsess over them to the point that you cannot let go of the distorted thoughts and begin to change your behavior based on them that anxiety disorder is the result. The goal of cognitive therapy, understanding how these thoughts are in error helps the patient let go of them and replace them with more positive thoughts and emotions, simultaneously allowing the patient to modify destructive behaviors, such as avoidance.

CBT, or cognitive-behavioral therapy, is an active therapy that seeks to modify both the destructive thought patterns and the resultant behavior. It is a proven therapy for panic disorder, GAD, OCD, SAD, PTSD and specific phobias. Some mental health professionals will require a patient to undergo this type of therapy before prescribing medications.

Other Treatment

According to WebMD, conventional medicine is beginning to include some treatment that alternative medicine relies upon. Dietary changes focus not only on nutritional support of the affected brain chemicals, but also on avoidance of certain foods or beverages that contain substances known to exacerbate anxiety symptoms. These include coffee, cola, energy drinks and chocolate.

Relaxation therapy seeks to calm the mind and body, in the belief that anxiety feeds upon itself. Techniques might include yoga, meditation or guided imagery. As stress melts away, the theory is that lowered stress means lowered anxiety as well.

More about both of these therapies in later sections.

Natural Treatment Options

Natural treatment options for anxiety include substances that reduce the symptoms of anxiety, nutritional support for brain chemistry, and calming techniques such as those discussed in the previous section. We will explore these options now.

Natural Medicines

Three natural herbs have received considerable attention as alternatives to conventional medication. They are Kava, valerian and passionflower. Other herbal medications are panax ginseng and St. John's Wort.

Kava

Kava, also known as kava-kava, is derived from a root that grows in the Pacific region. It is culturally important to the natives of islands in the regions, used in rituals and ceremonies. Consuming kava may induce mild euphoria or sedation, have an enhancing effect on social interaction or produce a numbing effect when used topically. Although traditional use involved various preparations such as grinding the plant for a flour-like substance or brewing the roots, kava is now available as a supplement in pill or extracts form. The active ingredients of kava are compounds known as kavalactones, which have an effect similar to the benzodiazepine class of medication. Numerous studies show that these compounds are effective against anxiety and may be less addictive and have fewer side effects than conventional medications. However, other studies have indicated a concern about liver damage, leading some European countries to ban it and the National Center for Complementary and Alternative Medicines (NCCAM) to suspend funding for some studies. Although it is currently not banned in the US, the NIH cites the following side effects and warnings: it can cause liver damage, including hepatitis and liver failure; it has been associated with several cases of dystonia (abnormal muscle spasm or involuntary muscle movement). In addition, long-term or heavy use may result in scaly or yellowed skin. Because of its sedative effect, users must avoid driving or operating heavy machinery. Kava may also interact with several drugs, including those used for Parkinson's disease. If you decide to try kava for your symptoms, you must inform your doctor so that he can make you aware of any drug interactions or other contraindications, such as existing liver disease.

Valerian

Valerian is thought to reduce stress in social situations, thereby easing anxiety. Studies have been inconclusive, however. Since valerian is likely safe for most people in short-term usage, it may be best just to try it. Long-term safe usage is unknown, but clinical trials lasting up to 28 days have shown medicinal amounts to be safe. There are some contraindications, though. There is not enough data to determine whether using valerian during pregnancy or breast-feeding is safe, so you should discontinue valerian in these cases. Additionally, since valerian is a central nervous system depressant, you should stop taking it at least two weeks before a scheduled surgery when you will be receiving a general anesthetic.

Valerian also has some side effects. Some people report headache, sluggishness or uneasiness, while others report excitability or insomnia. Until you know how it affects you, it is best not to drive or operate heavy machinery while taking valerian. Avoid possible side effects of discontinuing valerian after long-term use by reducing the dose slowly over a week or two.

Passionflower

Passionflower is prepared in extract and tablet form and has been shown in some studies to be as effective as prescription medications in reducing anxiety, particularly GAD. Dosage is 45 drops of extract by mouth per day for generalized anxiety disorder, or one 90-mg. tablet per day. Passionflower is a sedative, so it should not be used with other sedative medications, including anesthesia. Its safety with regard to pregnancy and breastfeeding has not been evaluated.

Passionflower also has some side effects, including confusion, dizziness, altered consciousness and irregular muscle action and coordination, as well as inflamed blood vessels. More rarely reported are nausea, vomiting, drowsiness, rapid heart rate and heart arrhythmia. The latter side effects may be related to allergic reaction, however.

Panax Ginseng

Panax ginseng has been used medicinally for over 2000 years, and its uses are many and varied, ranging from the treatment of anxiety and depression to breast cancer, diabetes and premature ejaculation. It has numerous active ingredients, which accounts for the broad spectrum of usage, and is often referred to as a general well-being medication.

With regard to anxiety, panax ginseng helps improve thinking and concentration, as well as helping to cope with stress. There is insufficient evidence to prove effectiveness in improving mood and the sense of well-being. Unfortunately, the list of substances, medications and health conditions with which ginseng panax interacts negatively is very long, and includes alcohol and caffeine as well as medications for diabetes, blood pressure and immunosuppressants. You should not take it if you have a heart condition, autoimmune disorder, bleeding conditions, diabetes, hormone-sensitive conditions such as certain types of cancer, organ transplant, insomnia, or schizophrenia. Otherwise, short-term use in adults is considered possibly safe. Researchers believe that the active substances in ginseng panax have hormone-like properties, making long-term use possibly unsafe.

The most common side effect is insomnia. More rarely, people report menstrual problems, vaginal bleeding or breast pain; high or low blood pressure, dizziness or increased heart rate; headache, loss of appetite, diarrhea, itching, rash and mood changes.

St. John's Wort

St. John's Wort is best known for treatment of depression, but has also been studied in relation to treatment for anxiety. Recent announcements have cast doubt on its effectiveness for the latter; however, some people still report relief from anxiety. If you can consider road rage a form of anxiety, the author can personally attest to the efficacy of St. John's Wort (on a friend) in alleviating the symptoms.

St. John's Wort usually does not induce side effects, although anxiety, dry mouth, sensitivity to sunlight, dizziness, stomach upset, headache, sexual problems, or fatigue are occasionally reported. However, it does interact with a variety of medications, including antidepressants, birth control pills, blood thinners, medicines for HIV, cancer drugs, cyclosporine, or digoxin

Conclusion

All of these natural substances have pros and cons. Just because a substance is natural does not mean it is not habit-forming, has no side effects or is not dangerous. In addition, since all of them act on the same brain chemicals as prescription medications, drug interactions are not only possible but also likely. It is imperative that you consult both your doctor and your pharmacist if you wish to try these substances in lieu of prescription medications.

Integrative, Alternative or Holistic Approaches

Although they differ in method and focus, anxiety is one condition for which conventional and alternative medical disciplines share some agreement. In conventional treatment, psychotherapy seeks to help the individual understand the causes of his anxiety and to alleviate it by challenging those beliefs and behaviors. Alternatively, and sometimes in conjunction with psychotherapy, conventional medicine utilizes medications to alter the balance of the brain chemicals that produce the emotions and physical symptoms of anxiety. Natural medicine has the same goals of balancing the mind and body, but adds spiritual balance to the mix. Modalities include hydrotherapy, hypnotherapy, meditation, nutritional therapy and a number of more specialized and esoteric therapies.

Hydrotherapy

Immersion in water is one of the time-honored methods of relaxation around the world. Just thinking about sinking into a warm tub of water induces a feeling of euphoria for some people. When the mind and body are relaxed, you can feel the anxiety ebbing away. This can be combined with aromatherapy or soothing herbs and essential oils in the water to further lighten mood, promote relaxation and relieve stress and anxiety. Ideally, the water should be between 100□ and 102□ Fahrenheit. The warm water slows down internal organs and promotes sleep, which is important in reducing anxiety.

Formal hydrotherapy involves a therapist and various exercises depending on the condition.

Hypnotherapy

Hypnotherapy is effective in treating a number of ailments, and anxiety is no exception. While in hypnotic trance, the patient's mind is open to suggestion, including the suggestion that the object of fear is not fearful after all. That being the case, hypnotherapy is particularly effective for phobias, social anxiety and PTSD. A trained hypnotherapist usually assists, but self-hypnosis after the patient receives training in the specific exercise can also help reinforce the changes in thinking or behavior that the patient desires.

Meditation

This catch-all word can be tossed out casually as a method of relaxation and anxiety treatment, but there are several different disciplines, including transcendental meditation, mindful meditation, and certain aspects of yoga. All are effective in achieving relaxation if correctly practiced, but studies have indicated that people who suffer from anxiety disorders may not be able on their own to achieve the state of relaxation required for efficacy. Meditation has not been shown to be superior in treating anxiety to other methods of relaxation. Nevertheless, for those who are able to achieve the desired state of mind and for whom the relaxation reduces anxiety, it is at least a safe alternative to consider. There is growing scientific evidence that meditation is effective, and why.

Transcendental Meditation

Transcendental meditation is the traditional form of meditation, brought to the consciousness of the masses in the late 1960s when the Beatles became interested in the teachings of Maharishi Mahesh Yogi, travelling in 1968 to India to attend an advanced training session in TM. The practice involves focusing the mind on an object until the practitioner's mind achieves stillness. Health benefits claimed by http://www.tm.org/ include reduced high blood pressure, reduced medication for high blood pressure, reduced atherosclerosis and thickening of the coronary arteries, reduced myocardial ischemia, reduced hospital rates and decreased medical care utilization, decreased anxiety, and reduced alcohol abuse. Numerous studies on these claims have produced conflicting results, but no one questions that TM reduces anxiety, assuming the patient is able to practice it properly.

Mindfulness Meditation

Mindfulness meditation is the practice of developing awareness of both external and internal experiences without judgement. This allows the practitioner to take note of physical and emotional responses but remain disengaged and regulate the response, rather than reacting emotionally or even analytically. It works by changing your thought processes; you are trained to observe without reacting, which over time allows you to be de-conditioned to negative thoughts, emotions and experiences. Instead of responding or trying to understand, you break the connection between the anxious thoughts and your physical response (panic symptoms, for example). Similar in effect to CBT, mindfulness meditation is in fact used in therapeutic treatment. Studies have shown that an eight-week course of study has been effective in significantly reducing anxiety, and that the benefits continue at a three-year follow-up examination.

Most recently, researchers at Wake Forest Baptist Medical Center published a study wherein the brain regions activated by mindfulness meditation were identified. They found that the areas associated with meditation-related anxiety relief were the anterior cingulate cortex, ventromedial prefrontal cortex and anterior insula. These areas are involved with executive function and the control of worrying.

Massage

Assuming the individual's anxiety disorder does not involve fear of another person being too close or touching her, massage can be an effective therapy for GAD, in particular. It can promote feelings of relaxation and physical relief from tension, and can lower cortisol levels, according to one theory. A clinical trial is underway to explore the effects of Swedish massage versus light-touch massage in a broad spectrum of anxiety disorder. "Preliminary studies suggest that massage therapy decreases symptoms of anxiety and depression, and lowers salivary cortisol levels in a wide array of childhood and adult neuropsychiatric disorders including post-traumatic stress disorder, attention-deficit-disorder hyperactivity, depression, bulimia and anorexia-nervosa." The study abstract goes on to state that the vast majority of GAD sufferers do not receive adequate pharmacotherapy or psychotherapy, indicating that this complementary or alternative therapy would be of benefit.

Other Therapies

Environmental Medicine, Light Therapy, Magnetic Field Therapy, Naturopathic Medicine, Orthomolecular Medicine and Traditional Chinese Medicine all fall into the category of alternative modalities that may or may not be effective. There is sufficient anecdotal evidence that each of them has provided relief for at least some people, but not enough clinical studies to meet the rigorous requirements of scientific proof. Qualified professionals trained in their use must perform these therapies.

How to calm the mind and body

Although many forms of anxiety disorder are both chronic and severe, people who have milder cases of some anxiety, or who experience it only rarely, may benefit from some self-care modalities. In addition, these hints can benefit more severe cases when used in conjunction with other treatment, always recognizing that it is necessary to consult with the doctor or therapist treating the patient before adding self-care, to prevent interaction.

Perhaps the simplest form of self-care involves learning some of the relaxation techniques that can reduce the physical distress of anxiety. Prayer, meditation, biofeedback, progressive relaxation, guided imagery, yoga, Qigong and self-hypnosis can all be effective to facilitate deep relaxation, calming both mind and body. It is important to practice one or more of these techniques daily, to maintain a manageable level of stress and prevent anxiety attacks. Which technique you will practice depends on your own ability to learn which works best for you.

Some of these techniques can even provide a mechanism to stop the physical responses to an anxiety attack even as it starts.

Prayer

For people of faith, prayer is the most natural activity, especially when a disturbing event or mental image occurs. It is very comforting to turn to a higher power for help, forgiveness and intervention. Consider also the positive mental effect of gratitude, another objective of prayer. In addition, it has been demonstrated that the focused prayer of others on behalf of the sufferer can have a beneficial effect. Do not discount the benefit that the sufferer would receive from praying for others. Focusing one's attention outside, rather than dwelling on one's own problems, is a proven mood lifter. Prayer promotes a positive outlook, which is very important to the mental health of anyone, no less so for the anxiety sufferer.

Meditation

There are at least two major schools of meditation, and one form of yoga includes a meditative form of breathing known as pranayama. While achieving a meditative state may be difficult for someone with anxiety disorder, these breathing exercises are not difficult, nor do they require beginning with a calm mind. Rather, they have the effect of calming both mind and body. However, they do require practice. Once you have mastered the techniques, try using one when you sense an anxiety attack coming.

Bellows Breath

Breathe in deeply through your nostrils. Allow your diaphragm to expand and force your abdomen outward, then fill your lungs and finally your collarbones rising as your chest expands. Now force your breath out quickly, again through your nostrils, emptying lungs and diaphragm both much more quickly than you breathed in. Beginners should begin slowly to avoid hyperventilation, but as you continue to practice, you can work up to a rapid breathing cycle. Continue repeating this cycle for 5 minutes.

Shining Forehead Breath

This technique is very similar to the previous one, but the focus is on exhaling very forcefully, assisting by rapidly pulling in your stomach muscles to expel the air. Do not force the exhalation to the point of discomfort, however.

Continue this exercise for 15 minutes, but you may rest one minute between each five-minute interval.

Alternate Nostril Breath

Close your eyes to focus your attention on your breathing. With your right thumb, press against your right nostril to close it. Slowly inhale through the left nostril only, filling your diaphragm and then your lungs. Remove your thumb from the right nostril, but do not exhale yet. Now use your ring and middle finger to completely block your left nostril, and exhale slowly and completely. Keeping your left nostril blocked, repeat the process with your right nostril. This completes one round. Continue for 15 minutes, resting for one minute between each five-minute interval if you wish. You may also switch hands if your arms get tired.6

External Breath

For this exercise, return to the practice of Bellows Breath, except that once you have exhaled, you will touch your chin to your chest and then suck your stomach in completely. Try to leave a hollow below your ribcage. Now hold the position as well as holding your breath as long as is comfortable. As you practice, you should be able to hold your breath for longer. When you must inhale, lift your chin and breathe in slowly to repeat the process. Repeat 3 to 5 times.5

Bee Breath

Close your eyes to focus on your breathing. Arrange your hands as follows: thumbs in ears, index fingers above eyebrows and remaining fingers along the sides of your nose, keeping each little (pinky) finger near a nostril. Breathe in deeply through the nostrils, using your diaphragm and then your lungs to fill your chest completely. Use the pinky fingers to close each nostril partially, while keeping your lungs filled. Now breathe out through the nose while humming within your throat. This will produce a soft buzzing through your nostrils as you exhale, hence the name of the exercise. Repeat three times.

Chanting Breath

This is the exercise that people who are not particularly familiar with yoga associate with it, and which is often spoofed in standup comedy, movies and TV. Nevertheless, it is a relaxation technique that is easy to perform. Breathe in deeply through your nose as with the first two exercises.

Exhale very slowly while saying Om. The objective is to allow the word to last as long as the exhale, keeping the O long and the M short. In other words, it should sound like OOOOOOOOOOOOOm, rather than Ommmmmmmmmm. Repeat three times.

If you have attempted these exercises as you read, you will see that it requires great focus on the exercise itself, leaving no room for fearful thoughts. While you may not wish to call attention to yourself in a public place if a panic attack is imminent, in the privacy of your home these would be very effective to forestall an attack.

Diaphragmatic Breathing

Another breathing exercise is diaphragmatic breathing. This also promotes relaxation as well as giving you something else to think about besides your fear or anxiety. To practice this technique, find a quiet and comfortable place to sit or lie down. Place your feet slightly apart, and Place one hand on your abdomen near your navel. Place the other hand on your chest. Inhale through your nose and exhale through your mouth. Concentrate on your breathing; notice which hand is rising and falling with each breath. Now gently exhale most of the air in your lungs. Inhale while slowly

73

counting to four. As you inhale, slightly extend your abdomen, causing it to rise about 1 inch. Make sure that you are not moving your chest or shoulders. As you breathe in, imagine the warmed air flowing in. Imagine this warmth flowing to all parts of your body. Pause for one second, and then slowly exhale to a count of four. As you exhale, your abdomen should move inward. As the air flows out, imagine all your tension and stress leaving your body.

As mentioned above in previous sections, both transcendental meditation and mindfulness meditation can also be effective in reducing anxiety. In particular, mindfulness meditation trains you to dispassionately observe a stimulus and then alter your physical and emotional response. For example, you might notice as you approach the podium to make a public address that your hands are shaking. Rather than giving way to the emotional response and succumbing to a panic attack, you would note the anxiety but not react to it. Because a panic attack involves a feedback loop that spirals from fear of the stimulus to fear of the physical symptoms of fear, the ability to remain calm and not react interrupts that process and averts the spiral of panic.

Progressive Relaxation

One of the most popular techniques for producing the relaxation response is progressive relaxation. This technique is often used in the treatment of anxiety and insomnia. Central to the concept is the idea that you have to first learn and experience the sensation of relaxation. Therefore, this technique teaches you what it feels like to relax by comparing relaxed to muscles with tensed muscles. Essentially, the technique requires you to contract a muscle for one to two seconds and then slowly relax it to feel the difference. It is best for you to lie down in a quiet place or sit in a comfortable chair in a room with soft lighting, feet flat on the floor, eyes closed. Then, go progressively through all the muscles of the body starting with your facial muscles and working your way down to your feet, slowly contracting, holding the contraction for a period of at least one to two seconds and then relaxing the muscles. Eventually you will find yourself in a deep state of relaxation.

Here is a more detailed description; follow along one step at a time.

Concentrate on your face, feeling any tension in your face and eyes. Begin by contracting the muscles of your face and neck, holding the contraction for a period of at least one to two seconds and then relaxing the muscles.

Make a mental picture of this tension-such as a rope tied in a knot or a clenched fist-and then mentally picture it being untied or relaxing and becoming comfortable, lying limp, like a relaxed rubber band.

Experience the feeling of your face and eyes becoming relaxed. As they relax, feel a wave of relaxation spreading throughout your body. Next, contract and relax your upper arms and chest, followed by your lower arms and hands.

Repeat the process progressively down your body: abdomen, buttocks, thighs, calves, and feet. Follow the same procedures and visualization techniques as described above. Mentally picture the tension in each part of the body, then picture the tension melting away; tense the area and then relax it.

While doing this take in deep breaths and mentally say, as you let out each breath, "Relax."

Repeat the whole sequence two or three times. After relaxing each part of your body, rest quietly in this comfortable state for two to five minutes. Now, prepare to open your eyes and become aware of the room, finally, let your eyes open. You should now be ready to continue with the day's activities, refreshed and relaxed. Practicing this technique in bed just before sleep is an effective anti-insomnia exercise as well.

Biofeedback and Neurotherapy Training

Although you must seek the services of therapists to learn these techniques, once you learn them, you will be able to practice them to reduce and prevent anxiety and panic attacks.

Biofeedback training involves the use of visual or auditory signals from a machine that records the responses from your body. By undergoing this training, you can learn to voluntarily relax specific muscles, alter your brain's electrical activity, reduce heart rate and blood pressure, increase body warmth and even improve gastrointestinal function. To facilitate the training, electrodes are placed on your skin (this is a simple and painless process) and you will then use various techniques, such as meditation and/or relaxation and visualization to affect the desired response (muscle relaxation, lowered heart rate etc). The biofeedback device reports your progress through the change in the speed of the beeps or flashes. As you become more and more successful in controlling the physical response, it actually subtly programs your body/and mind to control that response. Eventually you will be able to apply the techniques you used to affect the response, without the need for the machines to tell you of your success.

Neurotherapy is an extension of biofeedback and is used to reprogram your dominant brain w wave patterns (beta, alpha, theta, delta), bringing them into an optimal state of harmony and dynamic functioning. The benefit of this reprogramming is that permanent changes takes place, entirely independent of the conscious self-regulation skills gained via biofeedback.

Guided Imagery

While the word "guided" implies the presence of a therapist or other person to assist in directing your relaxation, there are also many programs on recorded media that can assist you in the privacy of your home. The idea is to have you in a comfortable position, eyes closed, as you proceed through an exercise of positive mental images designed to make your body relax as your mind also relaxes. Typically, these programs use soothing music and a soft voice suggesting what you should be imagining. They may also have subliminal beats that induce brain waves to conform to a relaxed state, which has the added advantage of positively altering the brain chemistry.

Yoga

The proper practice of yoga requires training, but can be accomplished on your own once you understand and perfect the exercises in a class. In an article dated April, 2009 Harvard Health Publications reported that, "Available reviews of a wide range of yoga practices suggest they can reduce the impact of exaggerated stress responses and may be helpful for both anxiety and depression. In this respect, yoga functions like other self-soothing techniques, such as meditation, relaxation, exercise, or even socializing with friends." The article goes on to describe how this occurs, and cites a study that indicated yoga can be an effective treatment for PTSD. It is well worth the read.

Laughter

American journalist, author, researcher and peace activist Norman Cousins advocated laughter as an anesthetic, incorporating it into his self-help regimen in fighting numerous illnesses. Cousins survived years longer than his doctors predicted, somewhat proving his own theories. As Adjunct Professor of Medical Humanities for the School of Medicine at the University of California, Los Angeles, Cousins further researched the biochemistry of human emotions, which he believed was a key to physical as well as mental health. Laughter can be an effective self-care tool. An ability to laugh at a situation, problem, or even ourselves, gives us a feeling of power. Humor and laughter can foster a positive and hopeful attitude and we are less likely to succumb to feelings of depression and helplessness if we are able to laugh at anxiety-producing situations.

Light

By now, most people understand the role of light in seasonal affective disorder. However, were you aware that light boosts serotonin production? That is the mechanism for the mood-lifting effects of light therapy. Whether you simply increase the exposure you have to the natural sunlight, or you must obtain a special light that is designed to mimic the sun's mix of light waves, it can help with anxiety when used with other therapies.

Lifestyle Changes

Far from meaning you should avoid all situations that produce anxiety, lifestyle change means that you must develop positive coping mechanisms. The fear that lies at the root of anxiety disorder, while possibly once valid, is now controlling your life. To overcome it requires mental courage as well as learning the physiological basis of emotion. To some extent, the simple act of resolving to be more positive can greatly reduce feelings of anxiety. One individual, bereft of many of her medications because of a move across state lines and the need to find a new doctor to prescribe them, found the courage after a suicide attempt to fight her anxiety with a positive attitude, saying, "God gave me another chance at life... I'm going to seize it by the horns." Her progress, in a very short few weeks was nothing short of miraculous, going from a 16-year battle with agoraphobia to the ability to sit outside her apartment door and watch her young relatives swimming in the pool—without anti-anxiety medication.

As we started the exploration of the treatment of anxiety disorder with drug therapy, let us now explore the brain chemistry that those drugs are designed to modify, and the role that diet and nutrition play in affecting brain chemistry.

Diet

As we learned in the discussion of meditation, there are several regions of the brain that either influence anxiety or directly contribute to it. The amygdala, associated with emotions, coordinates the body's response to fear. The cerebral cortex shapes the response to fear by evaluating data about a perceived threat and forming judgements about it. The prefrontal complex is involved in complex reasoning and decision-making, thus modulating social behavior. The hippocampus processes emotions and long-term memories, and the locus ceruleus helps decide whether a stimulus deserves attention. All of these processes and the communication between them rely on neurotransmitters, the messengers of the brain. The generation within the body of neurotransmitters, in turn, is highly interdependent with diet.

Neurotransmitters are divided into two types, inhibitory and excitatory. Serotonin and GABA are inhibitors. They make us feel good and are responsible for our self-esteem and sleep. If they are depleted, the result is depression, insomnia, and even anger. This is the basis for treatment of depression as well as anxiety with SSRIs, tricyclic antidepressants, SNRIs and benzodiazepines. A high-carbohydrate diet or a protein deficiency causes depletion of these neurotransmitters, as does stress, consumption of caffeine and ironically, several anti-depressant drugs including benzodiazepines.

Glutamate, catecholamines, PEA, and dopamine are excitatory. They are responsible for alertness, clear thinking, focus, memory, ambition, and stress. Other drug therapies rely on reducing norepinephrine, which can cause both panic and insomnia if overproduced. Stress is the major cause of norepinephrine overproduction, although it can also be caused by a tumor on the central core of the adrenal medulla. Although overproduction of norepinephrine results in these undesirable condition, underproduction or depletion can cause their own problems.

The key is balance. We require these neurotransmitters in the right balance if we are to feel well and be healthy. One of the reasons that medications for their regulation must be constantly adjusted is that the receptor sites for them work like those for insulin. Have you ever heard of insulin resistance? It is a response your body has to constant overproduction of insulin; the receptor sites develop a mechanism known as desensitization—essentially, they put up a 'closed for business' sign and refuse to accept more, a precursor to full-blown diabetes. Just as in insulin resistance, diet plays a crucial role in desensitization and depletion of brain chemicals.

Nutrients found in foods are precursors to neurotransmitters. That means that the body breaks down the foods into their separate chemical or elemental components, and then uses them to build the chemicals that the body needs to perform its functions. Depending on the amount of the precursors that are present in the food you consume, more or less of these chemicals, including neurotransmitters, are produced. Unfortunately, the process is not as straightforward as it seems, as it is complicated first by the fact that foods are more often than not made up of more than one nutrient, with varying levels of chemical components. Not only does the interaction of the various nutrients within the food itself influence the production and release of neurotransmitters, but also how each individual's body breaks the food down has an impact. Malfunction of one body system can lead to improper digestion and breakdown of a critical component for another system's chemicals.

Therefore, although we can list foods that will support production of the three important neurotransmitters for relief of anxiety, it is critical that you also pay attention to all other body systems to maintain the best health possible for the optimum results in consuming them. Following, we break down the dietary recommendations to support neurotransmitter production.

Serotonin

Serotonin deficiency can cause obsession and panic attacks, among other symptoms ranging from depression to irritability. It is the main cause of seasonal affective disorder, or 'winter blues'. Common wisdom concerning boosting serotonin is that eating foods high in the amino acid tryptophan will automatically boost serotonin; unfortunately, this is false. Tryptophan is a relatively small component of most foods containing it; therefore, it must compete with other, more bioavailable, amino acids in crossing the blood brain barrier. However, there are some recommendations that can make a difference.

First, avoid simple carbohydrates in favor of complex ones. Simple carbohydrates, like white sugar, white flour, processed cereals, white rice and other highly processed foods cause a spike in insulin production and a resulting 'low'. This cycle depletes serotonin. Your body absorbs complex carbohydrates more slowly, preventing the extremes of insulin response and conserving serotonin. Complex carbohydrates are whole grains, legumes and starchy vegetables like sweet potatoes and parsnips. Perhaps it is no coincidence that these foods also contain significant amounts of protein. Oatmeal, the old-fashioned kind, is particularly high in tryptophan, but most whole grains have some.

Next, eat healthy fats containing Omega-3 fatty acids. This polyunsaturated fat is essential for many body processes, and it has become deficient in the typical American diet as we have turned more and more to processed foods. Good sources of Omega-3 fatty acids are fish, especially cold-water fish like salmon and mackerel; in addition, nuts, seeds and seed oils are high in Omega-3s.

Believe it or not, dark chocolate is a serotonin-boosting food. And you thought you just loved the taste! The mechanism for this effect is resveratrol, which boosts endorphins as well as serotonin levels. Avoid milk chocolate, as it contains far less cocoa and the milk solids interfere with digestion of the healthful components. Choose the highest level of cocoa you can tolerate, and enjoy in moderation.

Finally, avoid the temporary stimulants caffeine, alcohol and sugar. Each of these substances provides a temporary lift, but then has a rebound effect. They actually deplete valuable hormones and brain chemicals, serotonin among them. If you must indulge, do so in limited quantities, no more than two cups of coffee or alcoholic drinks per day. Most medical practitioners suggest avoiding sugar (that is, processed sugars) altogether. Sweeten your foods with natural, unprocessed foods (like honey) instead, but again use in moderation.

Norepinephrine

Norepinephrine production depends on an adequate intake of the amino acid tyrosine, a major component of protein-rich foods. Other nutrients are involved; however maintaining adequate levels of tyrosine is the major concern in boosting norepinephrine. Not surprisingly, a list of foods that boost norepinephrine levels reads like the description of a balanced diet: high-quality proteins such as fish, lean meat and poultry, whole grains, dairy products, fruits, legumes, vegetables and nuts.

Specific foods that are high in either tyrosine or the co-agents that produce norepinephrine include the following:

Fish and seafood, meat and poultry: shrimp, tuna, cod, haddock, Pollock, lobster, snapper, pork, lean beef, wild game, chicken and turkey. Eggs also contain a high level of tyrosine.

Whole grains: Wheat and oats. In addition, wheat germ is high in phenylalanine, a precursor of tyrosine.

Dairy: Milk, cheese (cottage cheese, cream cheese, low fat cheddar cheese, parmesan cheese, provolone and mozzarella) and yogurt.

Fruits, vegetables and nuts: Lima beans, avocados, almonds, sesame seeds, pumpkin seeds and bananas are all high in tyrosine. Soy protein, tofu, peanut flour, seaweed, spinach, and beans also make the list.

GABA (Gamma-Aminobutryic Acid)

GABA is the neurotransmitter that is responsible for regulating the brain waves into calm, rhythmic alpha impulses, associated with relaxation and calm well-being. In addition, it inhibits beta impulses that contribute to a state of nervousness, racing thoughts and hyperactivity.

Foods that are helpful in the production of the GABA precursor glutamate are almonds, walnuts, other tree nuts, bananas, beef liver, broccoli, brown rice, halibut, lentils, oats, whole grain, oranges, citrus fruits, rice bran, spinach, whole wheat and other whole grains.

Perhaps you can see the pattern here. A well-balanced diet high in quality lean proteins, healthy fats, whole grains, some dairy products and a variety of fruits, vegetables seeds, nuts and legumes contributes to production of the neurotransmitters that affect anxiety. Processed foods do not.

Nutrition, supplements and herbs

For most people, getting the nutrition we need from the foods we eat is the most desirable course of action. However, what if we are unable to properly digest some of the best foods for our requirements, or are allergic to them? What if simply eating enough of them is a physical impossibility, like eating enough spinach to get the daily recommendation of iron (impossible because spinach also contains oxalates that block absorption, even if the massive quantities required did not deter you)? What if your reserves of the precursor nutrients are already so compromised or your stores of the neurotransmitters are so depleted that your body simply cannot catch up? In this case, you might consider the herbs previously discussed in the Natural Medicines section.

Other nutritional recommendations focus on supplemental support of several vitamins and minerals. Among them are the Vitamin B complex, known to stabilize the body's lactate levels, which are responsible for some types of anxiety attack. Clinical evidence suggests that one particular component, inositol (B8) is comparable in effectiveness to the SSRI fluvoxamine (Luvox; brand no longer available in the United States). Vitamin C in large doses produces a tranquilizing effect that reduces anxiety.

Trace elements important in the regulation of mood and anxiety include zinc, calcium, magnesium, potassium, and selenium. Calcium and magnesium prevent nervous tension when available in abundance. Magnesium relieves nervousness in addition to its acknowledged ability to relieve muscle spasms. Potassium is essential for the proper function of the adrenal system, responsible for the 'fight or flight' response that is overactive in anxiety sufferers. Selenium has been studied for its role in alleviating anxiety, one scholarly report citing its antioxidative role, "...the protective role of selenium in anxiety could be related to its important action in antioxidant defense." The paragraph goes on to state that oxidative damage to nerve endings leads to changes in neurotransmitter transport. Zinc is also known to generally calm the nervous system.

It is heartening to note that that a more natural approach to the relief of anxiety than drugs is receiving attention in more and more scholarly research. As research further explores the link between nutrition and the proper function of brain chemicals, the systems leading to their production, and the systems responsible for transporting them, hope for less dependence on dangerous drugs rises.

Animal Companionship

Not easily placed in the conventional/natural/self-care spectrum, the companionship of an animal must nevertheless be listed as something that can ease anxiety. For mild cases, an affectionate pet, whether it is a cat, a dog or some other type of animal can produce feelings of calm while you are physically close to it, for example, while petting it. A warm cat on your lap or a dog who nudges your elbow or hand to remind you to pet him evoke feelings of love and protection. Caring for an animal can take you out of your own thoughts and turn your attention to the needs of the pet instead. Even more focused are several categories of companion or service animals (mostly dogs) who are specially trained to provide emotional support or other services to individuals whose anxieties are more debilitating. These are Emotional Support Dogs, Skilled Companion Dogs and Mental Health Dogs.

Emotional support dogs (ESDs) are trained to provide comfort and security to people with special needs. They offer affection, an increased sense of purpose and decreased sense of isolation, mood improvement and increased social interaction, among other benefits.

Skilled Companion Dogs provide services for very specific needs, in addition to all the benefits of the ESDs. Each is specially trained for the needs of the person to whom they will eventually become a lifeline. A Skilled Companion Dog might be trained to alert a deaf owner to a ringing telephone or doorbell, remind an older person to take medication, or, as in the case of Tuesday, a PTSD Skilled Companion Dog mentioned earlier in this book, mitigate a flashback or panic attack by bringing his owner to the here and now. The latter is not just a loyal dog sensing that something is wrong with his master and investigating, as any dog would. These dogs are specially trained to take note of the physiological symptoms of a panic attack and to take specific actions in response. These dogs are meant for the benefit of patients whose quality of life would be improved, but who are too disabled to care for the dog themselves, or in some cases are too young or too old. For this reason, a facilitator, usually a parent, guardian or partner is required to take care of the animal's physical needs.

Mental Health Service Dogs are trained similarly to Skilled Companion Dogs and can provide similar services. However, these dogs are trained to provide companionship and all the other benefits of the other two types of trained dogs to persons over the age of 18. Individuals whose anxieties, mental disorders, developmental or intellectual disorders or other psychological conditions rise to the level of a disability could benefit from such a companion.

For more information on obtaining a trained animal of this type, or determining whether you or a loved one would qualify to receive one, use your favorite search engine and the phrase 'companion animal for anxiety.'

Conclusion

The obvious conclusion we must draw in our study of anxiety and its treatment is that both the condition and the treatment are divided into physical and mental components. As researchers continue to study the malfunction of brain chemistry that results in the physical symptoms as well as the emotions associated with anxiety, correcting that malfunction without the use of medication is becoming more and more feasible. On the other hand, dealing with the symptoms by retraining the patient's mind/body response promises relief even while we seek the cure of the underlying cause. We sincerely hope that you have learned something to give you hope in dealing with your own or a loved one's anxiety.

Bibliography

1. Encyclopedia of Natural Medicine Revised 2nd Edition: Michael Murray N.D. and Joseph Pizzorno N.D.

2. Alternative Medicine: The Definitive Guide; Second Edition: Larry Trivieri, JR Editor, Introduced by Burton Goldberg.

3. Alternative Cures: Bill Gottlieb

More Books by John McArtur

Hypothyroidism
Hypothyroidism: The Hypothyroidism Solution.
Hypothyroidism Natural Treatment and Hypothyroidism Diet for Under Active Or Slow Thyroid, Causing Weight Loss Problems, Fatigue, Cardiovascular Disease. John McArthur (Author), Cheri Merz (Editor)

Fibromyalgia And Chronic Fatigue
Fibromyalgia And Chronic Fatigue: A Step-By-Step Guide For Fibromyalgia Treatment And Chronic Fatigue Syndrome Treatment. Includes Fibromyalgia Diet And Chronic Fatigue Diet And Lifestyle Guidelines. John McArthur (Author), Cheri Merz (Editor)

Yeast Infection
Candida Albicans: Yeast Infection Treatment. Treat Yeast Infections With This Home Remedy. The Yeast Infection Cure. John McArthur (Author)

Heart Disease
Hypertension - High Blood Pressure: How To Lower Blood Pressure Permanently In 8 Weeks Or Less, The

Hypertension Treatment, Diet and Solution. John McArthur (Author)

Cholesterol Myth: Lower Cholesterol Won't Stop Heart Disease. Healthy Cholesterol Will. Cholesterol Recipe Book & Cholesterol Diet. Lower Cholesterol Naturally Keep Cholesterol Healthy. John McArthur (Author), Cheri Merz (Editor)

Heart Disease Prevention and Reversal: How To Prevent, Cure and Reverse Heart Disease Naturally For A Healthy Heart . John McArthur (Author)

Diabetes
Diabetes Diet: Diabetes Management Options. Includes a Diabetes Diet Plan with Diabetic Meals and Natural Diabetes Food, Herbs and Supplements for Total Diabetes Control. Delicious Recipes. John McArthur (Author), Corinne Watson (Editor)

Diabetes Cooking: 93 Diabetes Recipes for Breakfast, Lunch, Dinner, Snacks and Smoothies. A Guide to Diabetes Foods to Help You Prepare Healthy Delicious ... Diabetic Meals and Natural Diabetes Food) John McArthur (Author), Corinne Watson (Editor)

Stress and Anxiety
From Stressful to Successful in 4 Easy Steps: Stress at Work? Stress in Relationship? Be Stress Free. End Stress and Anxiety. Excellent Stress Management, Stress Control and Stress Relief Techniques. John McArthur (Author)

Anxiety and Panic Attacks: Anxiety Management. Anxiety Relief. The Natural And Drug Free Relief For Anxiety Attacks, Panic Attacks And Panic Disorder. John McArthur (Author), Cheri Merz (Editor)

Back and Neck Pain
The 15 Minute Back Pain and Neck Pain Management Program: Back Pain and Neck Pain Treatment and Relief 15 Minutes a Day No Surgery No Drugs. Effective, Quick and Lasting Back and Neck Pain Relief. John McArthur (Author)

Arthritis
Arthritis: Arthritis Relief for Osteoarthritis, Rheumatoid Arthritis, Gout, Psoriatic Arthritis, and Juvenile Arthritis. Follow The Arthritis Diet, Cure and Treatment Free Yourself From The Pain. John McArthur (Author)

Depression

How to Break the Grip of Depression: Read How Robert Declared War On Depression ... And Beat It! John McArthur (Author)

Pregnancy

Pregnancy Nutrition: Pregnancy Food. Pregnancy Recipes. Healthy Pregnancy Diet. Pregnancy Health. Pregnancy Eating and Recipes. Nutritional Tips and 63 Delicious Recipes for Moms-to-Be. Corinne Watson (Author), John McArthur (Author)

Pregnancy and Childbirth: Expecting a Baby. Pregnancy Guide. Pregnancy What to Expect. Pregnancy Health. Pregnancy Eating and Recipes. Cheri Merz (Author), John McArthur (Author)

Allergies

Allergy Free: Fast Effective Drug-free Relief for Allergies. Allergy Diet. Allergy Treatments. Allergy Remedies. Natural Allergy Relief. John McArthur (Author), Cheri Merz (Editor)

Made in the USA
Columbia, SC
13 May 2025

57871213R00062